Mammals of Mesa Verde National Park, Colorado

by Sydney Anderson

INTRODUCTION

A person standing on the North Rim of the Mesa Verde in southwestern Colorado sees a vast green plain sloping away to the south. The plain drops 2000 feet in ten miles. On a clear evening, before the sun reaches the horizon, the rays of the sun are reflected from great sandstone cliffs forming the walls of deep canyons that appear as crooked yellow lines in the distance. Canyon after canyon has cut into the sloping green plain. These canyons are roughly parallel and all open into the canyon of the Mancos River, which forms the southern boundary of the Mesa Verde. If the observer turns to the north he sees the arid Montezuma Valley 2000 feet below. A few green streaks and patches in the brown and barren low country denote streams and irrigated areas. To the northeast beyond the low country the towering peaks of the San Miguel and La Plata mountains rise more than 4000 feet above the vantage point on the North Rim at 8000 feet. To the northwest, in the hazy distance 90 miles away in Utah, lie the isolated heights of the La Sal Mountains, and 70 miles away, the Abajo Mountains.

In the thirteenth century, harassed by nomadic tribes and beset by years of drouth, village dwelling Indians left their great cliff dwellings in the myriad canyons of the Mesa Verde, and thus ended a period of 1300 years of occupancy. The story of those 1300 years, unfolded through excavation and study of the dwellings along the cliffs and earlier dwellings on the top of the Mesa, is one of the most fascinating in ancient America. To stop destructive commercial exploitation of the ruins, to preserve them for future generations to study and enjoy, and to make them accessible to the public, more than 51,000 acres, including approximately half of the Mesa, have been set aside as Mesa Verde National Park, established in 1906. The policies of the National Park Service provide protection, not only for the features of major interest in each park, but for other features as well. Thus the policy in Mesa Verde National Park is not only to preserve the many ruins, but also the wildlife and plants.

Five considerations prompted me to undertake a study of the mammals of Mesa Verde National Park: First, the relative lack of disturbance; second, the interesting position, zoogeographically, of the Mesa that extends as a spur of higher land from the mountains of southwestern Colorado and that is almost surrounded by arid country typical of much of the Southwest; third, the discovery in the Park of Microtus mexicanus, a species of the Southwest until then not known from Colorado; fourth, the co-operative spirit of the personnel at the Park when I visited there in 1955; and finally, the possibility of making a contribution not only to our knowledge of mammals, but to the interpretive program of the Park Service.

A Faculty Research Grant from The University of Kansas provided some secretarial help and field expenses for August and early September, 1956, when my wife, Justine, and I spent our vacation enjoyably collecting and studying animals in the Park. The co-operation of Dr. E. Raymond Hall is greatly appreciated; a grant to him from the American Heart Association provided field expenses for work by Mr. J.R. Alcorn, collector for The University of Kansas Museum of Natural History, in 1957.

Mr. Harold R. Shepherd of Mancos, Colorado (Senior Game Biologist for the State of Colorado, Department of Game and Fish), provided advice in the field, helped in identifying plants, and saved specimens of rodents (in 1958 and 1959) taken in his studies of the effect of rodents on browse utilized by deer. Mr. J.D. Hart, Assistant Director of the Department of Game and Fish, issued a letter of authority to collect in Colorado; and Superintendent O.W. Carlson approved my appointment as a collaborator. Mr. "Don" Watson, then Park Archeologist, and Mrs. Jean M. Pinkley, now Park Archeologist, assisted us in 1956, and since then have provided advice and assistance, and have reviewed the manuscript of this report.

Geologically, the Mesa Verde is the northern edge of a Cretaceous, coal-bearing, sandstone deposit called the Mesaverde group, which dips beneath the San Juan Basin of New Mexico. An abrupt retreating escarpment commonly forms on arid plateaus underlain by horizontal rocks of unequal strength, and characterizes the borders of mesas. Such an escarpment forms the North Rim of the Mesa Verde. However, the dip of the rocks has channelled drainage southward and erosion has cut numerous, deep, parallel-sided canyons rather than a simple, retreating escarpment. The Mesa Verde therefore is, technically speaking, a cuesta rather than a mesa. The remnants of the plateau left between the canyons are also (and again incorrectly in the technical sense) called mesas; Chapin Mesa and Wetherill Mesa are examples.

Climatically, the Mesa Verde is arid; precipitation averaged 18.41 inches per year for a period of 37 years. Precipitation may be scattered through the year, and more important, may be erratic from month to month and from year to year. In addition to low precipitation and periods of drouth, a great amount of sunshine, and thin, well-drained soils on all but the more sheltered parts of the Mesa favor vegetation that requires neither great amounts of, nor a continuous supply of, water.

The vegetation of the Mesa is illustrated in Plates 1 and 2, and consists predominantly of pinyon pine, Pinus edulis Engelm., and Utah juniper, Juniperus osteosperma (Torr.) Little. More sheltered areas along the North Rim and in most of the canyons support scattered small stands of Douglas fir, Pseudotsuga menziesii (Merb.) Franco. These are the "spruce trees" of Spruce Tree Canyon. An occasional ponderosa pine, Pinus ponderosa Laws., represents a vestige of more montane species of plants and animals in the Park. The dusky grouse, Dendragapus obscurus (Say), occurs along the North Rim in oak-chaparral, and is one of the few montane species of birds; several montane mammals are discussed later. The vegetation of the Mesa Verde has not changed appreciably in the last thousand years. The tree rings of 13 centuries show that Douglas fir has grown essentially as it does now, varying with precipitation from year to year, and periodically suffering from drouth (Schulman, 1946:18). Surface ruins yield mostly pinyon and juniper; cave ruins yield more Douglas fir than surface ruins; and "only rarely does yellow pine [Pinus ponderosa] occur in the ruins, indicating that then, as now, this tree grew only in the northern and higher parts of the Mesa Verde, remote from most of the ruins" (Getty, 1935:21).

Not all areas within the Park are undisturbed. The rights of way of roads are kept clear, as are campgrounds and other facilities in the area of headquarters. Part of the Mancos Valley within the Park is privately owned and is still in agricultural use. Cattle from land belonging to the Ute Indians wander into the Park from the Mancos Canyon along the floor of the canyon above the mouth of Weber Canyon. In addition to the pasture near headquarters, Prater Canyon below a fence across the canyon above Middle Well is used to pasture horses used by visitors to the Park and belonging to the pack and saddle concessioner. In 1956, the floor of Long Canyon was grazed by stock belonging to Utes, and horses ranged freely onto Wetherill Mesa as far as the North Rim. Occasionally livestock enter the floor of other canyons, for example Navajo, Soda, Prater, Morfield, and Waters canyons, owing to inadequate fencing, or no fencing.

The first mammals from the Mesa to be preserved for scientific study were seven specimens in the United States National Museum (designated USNM in lists of specimens examined) obtained by Merritt Cary in 1907, and mentioned in his "Biological Survey of Colorado" (Cary, 1911). In 1931 and 1932, R.L. Landberg obtained a few specimens that are in the Denver Museum of Natural History. In 1935, C.W. Quaintance, Lloyd White, Harold P. Pratt, and A.E. Borell prepared specimens, some of which remain in the museum at the Park (all specimens in the museum at the Park are designated by "MV" for Mesa Verde and by their catalogue numbers), and some are in the Museum of Vertebrate Zoology at the University of California at Berkeley (designated "MVZ" in the following accounts). Specimens in The University of Kansas Museum of Natural History are referred to by catalogue numbers only. Specimens prepared by D. Watson bear dates from 1936 until 1955. In 1938, Raymond F. Harlow prepared some specimens; his Student Technician's Report of 7 typescript pages, for July 8 to September 9, 1938, is on file at Mesa Verde National Park. In 1944 and 1945, Dr. D.A. Sutton, then a student at the University of Colorado, collected chipmunks for his own study, and also some other specimens that are in the University of Colorado Museum and the Park Museum. In 1949, Dr. R.B. Finley, then a student at The University of Kansas, collected in and near the Park and obtained a few specimens preserved in The University of Kansas Museum of Natural History. Rodents preserved by Harold R. Shepherd have been mentioned. I have examined 244 specimens that were collected by the above persons. Between August 8 and September 4, 1956, and on July 17, 1960, I collected 216 mammals from Mesa Verde National Park. Between November 3, and 12, 1957, J.R. Alcorn collected 275 mammals from the Mesa. The total of specimens examined is 735.

Written reports by C.W. Quaintance, H.P. Pratt, and R. Harlow have been of considerable use. A typescript report of 13 pages by Wildlife Technician H.P. Pratt for the period from September 9 to October 15, 1935, and monthly reports comprising 40 typescript pages and 4 pages with photographs by C.W. Quaintance for the period from February 18 through July 17, 1935, are on file at offices of Region Four, National Park Service, 180 New Montgomery Street, San Francisco 5, California. Chief Ranger Wade has kindly made available the files in his office, including reports of the Superintendent and reports of the Chief Ranger in earlier years, and Annual or Biennial Animal Census Reports since 1930. Special reports on prairie dogs, porcupines, and deer are in the files. These reports, and random reports that were regarded as reliable, are recorded on card files in both the Chief Ranger's office and Park Archeologist's office. Most of the information reported here on the larger mammals was gleaned from the above sources. A study of population fluctuations in porcupines by Donald A. Spencer and perhaps a study of movements of porcupines by Spencer, Wade and Fitch are to be published elsewhere. Other studies still in progress are mentioned in the following accounts.

ACCOUNTS OF SPECIES

Sorex merriami leucogenys Osgood Merriam's Shrew

Specimen: MV 7898/507, head of Navajo Canyon (locality No. 7 in Fig. 2), October 21, 1954.

This was the third reported specimen of the rare Merriam's shrew from Colorado (Rodeck and Anderson, 1956:436).

Sorex vagrans obscurus Merriam Wandering Shrew

Specimens examined.--Total, 8: Morfield Canyon, 7600 ft., 75972, 75973; Upper Well, Prater Canyon, 7575 ft., 69235-69238; 1/4 mi. N Middle Well, Prater Canyon, 7500 ft., 69239-69240.

The specimens from Prater Canyon were trapped in the grasses and sedges of the meadow comprising the floor of the canyon. The ground and vegetation were dry at the time of capture, September 2, 3, and 4, 1956. Microtus montanus was the only other species taken in the mouse traps in the sedge and grass. Five of the six specimens from Prater Canyon are young, having slightly worn teeth; the sixth is an old adult male the teeth of which are so much worn that only a few traces of the reddish-brown pigment remain. His testes were 5 mm. long. These specimens are from an area of intergradation between S. v. obscurus and S. v. monticola. The length of the maxillary tooth-row in these six specimens averaged 6.23 (6.1-6.4) millimeters. Comparison with average measurements of 6.6 and 6.8 in samples of S. v. obscurus, and of 5.9 in a sample of S. v. monticola (Findley, 1955:64, 65) reveals the intermediate size of the specimens from the Mesa Verde. The gap between habitat suitable for Sorex vagrans on the Mesa Verde and the nearest record-station for S. v. monticola to the south and west in the Chuska Mountains is wider than the gap between the Mesa Verde and the nearest record-station for S. v. obscurus to the north and east, one mile west of Mancos, 75971, 7000 feet, or at Silverton. On geographic grounds the specimens from the Mesa Verde are referred to S.

v. obscurus. The two specimens from Morfield Canyon were trapped on November 4, 1957, and are grayish above and silvery below. Their pelage contrasts markedly with the dorsally brownish and ventrally buffy pelage of the September-taken specimens from Prater Canyon.

Myotis californicus stephensi Dalquest California Myotis

Specimens examined.---Total, 3: Rock Springs, 7400 ft., 69243, 69246, August 21 and 22, 1956; 4505 Denver Museum, within the Park (exact locality not recorded), R.L. Landberg, July 27, 1931.

The specimens from Rock Springs were an adult male and a non-pregnant adult female. Both were shot over the road in pinyon and juniper. The specimens are referred to M. c. stephensi on account of their paleness, stephensi being paler than M. c. californicus from east of Mesa Verde in Colorado.

Myotis evotis evotis (H. Allen) Long-eared Myotis

Specimens examined.--Total, 4: Chickaree Draw, Prater Canyon, 8200 ft., MV 7841/507, probably in the summer of 1935; Rock Springs, 7400 ft., 69241, August 23, 1956, and 69249, August 18, 1956; Museum, Headquarters, 6950 ft., 69251, August 24, 1956.

An adult male (69241) was taken in a Japanese mist net stretched fifteen feet across a dirt road where it entered the stand of pinyon and juniper at the south edge of the burn on Wetherill Mesa between 7:20 and 8:30 p.m.; at the same place and time I captured five other bats of four species: Myotis thysanodes, Myotis subulatus, Eptesicus fuscus, and Plecotus townsendii. A piece of mist net attached to an aluminum hoop-net two and one half feet in diameter was used to good advantage in capturing bats rebounding from the larger mist net, and in frightening bats into the larger net when they approached closely. An adult male (69249) was shot at 7:20 p.m. while flying six to eight feet from the ground between pinyon trees up to 20 feet high; the air temperature was 70?F.

A female (69251) was found seemingly exhausted on the floor in the museum at Park Headquarters in the daytime, and was immature as indicated by small size, open basicranial sutures, unworn teeth, weakly ossified zygoma, and open epiphyseal sutures of phalanges.

Myotis subulatus melanorhinus (Merriam) Small-footed Myotis

Specimens examined.--Total, 8: Rock Springs, 7400 ft., 69242, 69244, 69245, 69247, 69248, August 21 to 23, 1956; Hospital, Park Headquarters, MV 7886/507, [Male], July 12, 1939; Headquarters, MV 7877/507, [Female], August 30, 1938; 4504 Denver Museum, within the Park (exact locality not recorded), R.L. Landberg, July 27, 1931.

The specimens from Rock Springs are two adult males that were shot, and one adult male, one adult female, and one young male that were netted at the place described in the account of Myotis evotis. The three adult males are near the average color of M. s. melanorhinus, and distinctly darker than the Myotis californicus from the Mesa Verde. In the female the pelage is paler and brighter, and the ears and membranes are darker, than in M. californicus.

Myotis thysanodes thysanodes Miller Fringed Myotis

Specimen: Rock Springs, 7400 ft., 69250, ad. [Female], August 23, 1956; taken in net as noted in account of Myotis evotis.

Myotis volans interior Miller Long-legged Myotis

Specimen: Rock Springs, 7400 ft., 69252, ad. [Female], August 21, 1956; shot over road.

Eptesicus fuscus pallidus Young Big Brown Bat

Specimen: Rock Springs, 7400 ft., 69253, ad. [Female], August 23, 1956; taken in net as noted in account of Myotis evotis.

Plecotus townsendii pallescens (Miller) Townsend's Big-eared Bat

Specimens examined.--Total, 5: Rock Springs, 7400 ft., 69254, ad. [Female], non-pregnant, August 23, 1956; Square Tower House, 6700 ft., 69255-69258, March, 1955.

The specimen from Rock Springs was taken in a net as noted in the account of Myotis evotis. The specimens from Square Tower House were obtained by D. Watson in a dimly lighted chamber formed by fracture in the rocks at the bottom of the canyon wall, above the talus slope. The bats were suspended from the wall of the chamber, which was at least six feet wide and fifteen feet long.

Tadarida brasiliensis mexicana (Saussure) Brazilian Free-tailed Bat

Specimens examined.--Total, 2: Cliff Palace, 6800 ft., MV 7862/507 and 7863/507, males, both collected by A.E. Borell, on August 23, 1936.

Lepus californicus texianus Waterhouse Black-tailed Jackrabbit

The black-tailed jackrabbit inhabits the Montezuma Valley to the north of the Mesa Verde and the Mancos Valley to the northeast, and has been seen occasionally on the top of the Mesa according to reports with date and locality noted in the files at the Park for the years 1941, 1942, 1947, 1948, 1950, and 1951. In 1942 four observations were made, in 1950 and 1951 two observations were recorded each year, and in other years only one observation was recorded each year. Nine observations are for Chapin Mesa south of Far View; only two observations are for higher elevations on the North Rim.

Sylvilagus audubonii warreni Nelson Desert Cottontail

Specimens examined.--Total, 2: Head of Prater Canyon, MV 7850/507; Far View Ruins, 75974, ad. [Female], non-pregnant, November 8, 1957.

One specimen was shot, while it was sitting near a pile of logs, by J.R. Alcorn by means of a bow and arrow. Although S. audubonii occurs on the Mesa along with S. nuttallii, S. audubonii is the species of the lowlands throughout the western United States at the latitude of Mesa Verde National Park. For example, S. a. warreni (69260) but not S. n. pinetis was obtained along the east side of the Mancos River at 6200 feet elevation (less than 50 yards outside the Park) and the same was true at the same elevation at a place 4-1/2 mi. N of the Park (No. 69259 from 2 mi. E Cortez).

Sylvilagus nuttallii pinetis (J.A. Allen) Nuttall's Cottontail

Specimens examined.--Total, 3: ad. [Male], 69263, skull only, dead on road, 1-3/4 mi. N Park Headquarters, 7275 feet, August 9, 1956; ad. [Female], 69261, no embryos, dead on road, 3/4 mi. S and 1-3/4 mi. W Park Point, 8000 ft, August 8, 1956; ad. [Male], 69262, shot in brushy area on the burn on Wetherill Mesa 2 mi. NNW Rock Springs, 7900 ft., August 24, 1956.

Nuttall's cottontail in Colorado is in general the cottontail of the highlands, and the three localities just mentioned are on the top of the Mesa Verde.

Sciurus aberti mimus Merriam Abert's Squirrel

Specimens examined.--Total, 2: [Male], MV 7872/507, prepared by D. Watson, killed by a car "near" the Park Well on September 24, 1937; [Female] (an unnumbered cased skin only), found dead "near" the Park Well on June 21, 1937.

Since 1934 these squirrels have been observed and recorded each year except in 1938, 1943, 1947, 1953, 1957, and 1958. The 77 reported observations can be grouped as follows: 11 from within a mile of the entrance to the Park, 14 from the North Rim or higher parts of canyons adjacent to it, 38 from Chapin Mesa south of Far View, and 14 not classifiable. The large number of observations on Chapin Mesa, chiefly in the vicinity of Park Headquarters, indicates the presence of more observers rather than more squirrels in this area.

Tamiasciurus hudsonicus fremonti (Audubon and Bachman) Red Squirrel

Specimens examined.--Total, 2: MV 7843/507, Chickaree Draw, Prater Canyon, 1935, C.W. Quaintance and Lloyd White; [Female], 69264, no embryos, 1/4 mi. NNW Middle Well, Prater Canyon, 7600 ft., August 31, 1956.

Red squirrels, or chickarees as they are called in Colorado, are known from only one place on the Mesa Verde, a side canyon on the west side of Prater Canyon above Middle Well. This side canyon has been named Chickaree Draw by C.W. Quaintance, who, with Lloyd White, studied the chickaree there in 1935. Quaintance reported the small colony at 7800 feet elevation in Douglas fir beneath which were found piles of cones from which the seeds had been eaten by the chickarees. On May 29, 1935, White observed a chickaree eating green oak leaves. On June 3, 1935, a nest was found in an old hollow snag up under the rim rock; there were four young squirrels in the nest. At least one nest was in a juniper and was composed mostly of oak leaves and grass. One nest twenty-five feet from the ground in a Douglas fir was composed of oak leaves and finely shredded cedar bark. In August, 1956, I found these squirrels in the same area and I shot one specimen. Other chickarees were seen and heard and the characteristic piles of parts of Douglas fir cones still attest to their presence. On September 1, 1953, D. Watson observed a pair of chickarees in Prater Canyon. The only other specific record in the files at the Park is of two seen in a branch of Soda Canyon in late 1956. Jean Pinkley tells me that chickarees have been observed in 1958 and 1959 at several other localities from Prater Canyon to the hill at the head of Navajo Canyon. The extent to which increased observations indicate an increase in number of chickarees is uncertain, since the amounts of time spent in the field and the percentage of observations recorded are not known.

Marmota flaviventris luteola A.H. Howell Yellow-bellied Marmot

Records are available of observations at 14 different places in the Park and in 19 different years between 1930 and 1960. Approximately two-thirds of the observations have been on Prater Grade or in upper Prater Canyon or in upper Morfield Canyon. On the morning of August 24, 1956, Harold Shepherd and I heard the whistle of an animal that he was certain was a marmot, 2 mi. NNW of Rock Springs at the west rim of Wetherill Mesa. Mr. Shepherd has worked in areas occupied by marmots for years in southwestern Colorado. Wetherill Mesa is the locality farthest west in the Park where marmots are known to occur. They occur as far south as Cliff Palace.

Cynomys gunnisoni zuniensis Hollister Gunnison's Prairie Dog

Specimens examined.--Total, 3: MV 7836/507, Prater Canyon, 7600 ft., C.W. Quaintance and L. White, May 24, 1935; [Female], MV 7847/507, head of Prater Canyon, June 13, 1935, C.W. Quaintance (the skin is on display); MV 7887/507, Prater Canyon, September 1, 1939.

C.W. Quaintance in reports on the results of his work in 1935 included the following information:

On February 20 in Prater Canyon Ranger Markley noticed that prairie dogs were active although about three feet of snow lay on the ground. Between April 15 and May 15 approximately 500 prairie dogs were in Prater Canyon above Lower Well; through field glasses 350 were counted. Young were first noted in Prater Canyon on July 12. Quaintance and Lloyd White had under observation two bulky nests of the red-tailed hawk in the tops of tall Douglas firs in side draws of Prater Canyon. Quaintance found near the rimrock a quarter of a mile from the prairie-dog town the skeletons of two prairie dogs between a sliver of a dead pinyon branch and the branch itself. Another skeleton lay on a dead limb fifteen feet from the ground. A red-tailed hawk once was observed to swoop down, seize a prairie dog and fly down the canyon. The four colonies found in the Park were in Prater Canyon, in Morfield Canyon, in the east fork of School Section Canyon, and in Whites Canyon. The last two were smaller colonies than the first two.

Prairie dogs were observed away from these colonies. On June 20 a young prairie dog ran into a culvert on the Knife Edge Section of the road. Others were observed on the north side of the road, at the head of the east prong of School Section Canyon, on the road west of Park Point, and on the road at the head of Long Canyon five miles from the nearest known colony in the Park. Possibly this last individual came from the Montezuma Valley north of the Park. Mr. Prater, after whom Prater Canyon is named, homesteaded on the Mesa Verde in 1899. He informed Quaintance that prairie dogs were present in Morfield Canyon prior to 1900 but were not in Prater Canyon in 1899. Prater said he drowned out a few that came into Prater Canyon before 1914. In 1942, Chief Ranger Faha wrote in his Annual Animal Census Report that he had interviewed an old time resident (name not noted) who stated that prairie dogs were not present on the Mesa Verde until about 1905 or 1906 and that Helen Morfield, the daughter of Judge Morfield who homesteaded in Morfield Canyon, brought the first prairie dogs on the Mesa Verde. Estimates of the prairie-dog population in the Annual Animal Census Reports for 1935 through 1941 were: 1935--800, 1936--650, 1937--650, 1938--650, 1939--no report, 1940--1500 and increasing, 1941--slight decrease. After 1942 more adequate records were kept by Chief Ranger Wade and other Park Service personnel.

On August 9, 1943, occupied burrows of prairie dogs were found to be thinly scattered down Prater Canyon from the head of the canyon at the Maintenance Camp to a point about one hundred feet below the lower well. The largest concentration was in the vicinity of the upper well near Prater's Cabin. Little new digging that would indicate a spreading population was noticed. Seemingly desirable, but unoccupied, habitat extended at least two miles south of the inhabited area. In Morfield Canyon, burrows were found from a point one hundred yards north of the fence at the south boundary of Section 17, south for a mile and one-half to a point one-third of a mile into Section 29. The greatest concentration was in the vicinity of Morfield Well. South of this point the burrows were found only along the narrow dry sides of the canyon and in sage-covered areas at slightly higher elevations than the rest of the floor of the canyon. Seemingly desirable habitat extended at least three miles to the south and one mile to the north of the occupied area. The report of the study in 1943 concluded with the statement that artificial control by poisoning would be unwise and unnecessary. Requests were being made at that time to exterminate prairie dogs in the Park on the basis of the unproved assumption that prairie dogs move from the Park to surrounding range land where extermination was then being attempted by poisoning.

On August 10, 1944, no occupied burrows were found in Whites Canyon or the east fork of School Section Canyon. A heavy rain on August 9 made accurate count of occupied burrows possible. In Prater Canyon the occupied area extended 200 feet south of the area occupied in 1943. In Morfield Canyon no change had occurred. North of the fence in Morfield Canyon 130 occupied burrows were counted. More than one hole, if judged to be part of the same burrow system, were counted as one. The vegetation within the colony had continued to improve in spite of the large population of prairie dogs.

On August 8 and 14, 1945, although a careful search was made, the only prairie dogs found in Prater Canyon were living in one burrow fifty yards from the Maintenance Camp. In Morfield Canyon the colony had decreased. Occupied burrows were found on the west side of the canyon near the fence and above the well (17 burrows), and below the well on the west side (estimated 30 burrows). The total population in both canyons was estimated to be 100, compared with 800 in the preceding year. The ground-water table was thought to be rising, and vegetation was increasing.

On August 12, 1946, two prairie dogs were observed in Prater Canyon, one near the Maintenance Camp, and the other a mile to the south. In Morfield Canyon 18 occupied burrows were found north of the fence and 36 below the well, in the same two areas occupied in 1945.

On August 12, 1947, two animals were seen at one of the localities occupied a year earlier in Prater Canyon, and three burrows were occupied. In Morfield Canyon 119 occupied burrows were counted. At least 12 dens occupied by badgers were present in 1946, and four in 1947.

On August 9, 1948, no evidence of living prairie dogs was found in Prater Canyon. In Morfield Canyon 45 burrows were counted north of the fence. The grass had been increasing in abundance for several years.

On August 18, 1949, no evidence of living prairie dogs was found in either canyon. In 1951 five prairie dogs were said to have been seen in Prater Canyon in June and July. No other observations have been recorded.

On June 22, 1956, 13 pups and 7 adult prairie dogs were released in an enclosure in Morfield Canyon. Periodic inspections in the summer revealed that the colony was surviving and healthy. By the following spring no prairie dogs remained. Another reintroduction is planned this year (1960).

Both the history of the prairie dogs and the history of the viewpoint of people toward them are interesting. Individual views have ranged from a desire to exterminate all the prairie dogs to a desire to leave them undisturbed by man.

In review: The early history of prairie dogs on the Mesa Verde is not well documented but reports are available of the absence of prairie dogs before settlement by white men, and of introductions of prairie dogs. Other reports indicate that prairie dogs have been observed far from established colonies; therefore natural invasion may account for the establishment of prairie dogs on the Mesa. Grazing of moderate to heavy intensity by livestock continued in Morfield Canyon until 1941. Cessation of grazing and above average precipitation were accompanied by increased growth of vegetation in the colonies of prairie dogs. Mr. Wade has suggested that flooding of burrows by ground water drove prairie dogs from some lower parts of the floors of the canyons, and that increased vegetation favored predators, primarily badgers and coyotes, which further reduced the population. The abruptness of the decline, especially in Prater Canyon, is consistent with the theory that some epidemic disease occurred. This possibility was considered at the time of the decline, and a Mobile Laboratory of the United States Public Health Service spent from June 5 to June 25, 1947, in the Park collecting rodents and their fleas for study. The primary concern was plague, which had been detected in neighboring states. No evidence of plague or of tularemia was reported after study of 494 small rodents obtained from 13 localities in the Park. Only six prairie dogs (all from Morfield Canyon) were studied. The negative report does not prove that tularemia or some other disease was not a factor in the decimation of the colony in Prater Canyon the year before.

If prairie dogs were able to survive primarily because of over-grazing by domestic animals, future introductions may fail. If disease was the major factor in their disappearance, reintroductions may succeed.

Spermophilus lateralis lateralis (Say) Golden-mantled Ground Squirrel

Specimens examined.--Total, 10: highway at School Section Canyon, MV 7894/507; Sect. 27, head of east fork of Navajo Canyon, 7900 ft., 69265; and Prater Canyon, 7600 to 7800 ft., MV 7835/507, 7837/507, 7846/507, 7874/507, 7875/507, MVZ 74411-74413.

In 1956, I observed S. lateralis 1/2 mi. W of Park Point, 3/4 mi. WSW Park Point, in the public campground at Park Headquarters, at the lower well in Prater Canyon, and at two other places on the North Rim. Other observations on file were made at Prater Grade, Park Point, "D" cut (on North Rim 1 mi. WSW Park Point), and Morfield Canyon. A juvenile was noted at Park Point on June 28, 1952, by Jean Pinkley, and five young were seen together at "D" cut on July 3, 1935. The earliest observation, also recorded by Jean Pinkley, was on February 1, 1947. All of the localities with the exception of Park Headquarters are above 7500 feet, and most of the localities are in vegetation that is predominantly oak-brush.

Spermophilus variegatus grammurus (Say) Rock Squirrel

Specimens examined.--Total, 6: Head of Prater Canyon, MV 7876/507; Chickaree Draw, Prater Canyon, MV 7843/507, 7844/507; Headquarters Area, MV 7888/507; Ruins Road 1/2 mi. NE of Cliff Palace, MV 7893/507; and

Spruce Tree House, 4334 in Denver Museum.

Specimen number 7893/507 had 360 Purshia seeds in its cheek-pouches according to a note on the label. On July 18, 1960, I found a young male rock squirrel dead on the road a mile north of headquarters that had 234 pinyon seeds in its cheek-pouches. Young, recorded as "half-grown," have been observed in May and July. The first appearance may be as early as January. In 1950, D. Watson thought that they did not hibernate, except for a few days when the weather was stormy. I observed a rock squirrel in August in the public campground at Park Headquarters sitting on its haunches on a branch of a juniper some twelve feet from the ground and eating an object held in its forefeet. The rock squirrel ranges throughout the Park in all habitats.

Eutamias minimus operarius Merriam Least Chipmunk

Specimens examined.--Total, 17: North Rim above Morfield Canyon, MV 7856/507; Morfield Canyon, 7600 ft. (obtained on Nov. 4, 1957), 75976; Middle Well in Prater Canyon, 7500 ft, MV 7855/507; Prater Canyon, 7600 ft., MVZ 74414; Park Point, 8525 ft., 69267-69270; 1/4 mi. S, 3/4 mi. W Park Point, 8300 ft., 69271-69272; Sect. 27, head of east fork of Navajo Canyon, 7900 ft., 69273; Far View Ruins, 7700 ft., 69274-69275, and two uncatalogued specimens in preservative; 3 mi. N Rock Springs, 8200 ft., 69276-69277.

Five of the fourteen specimens of known sex are females, all of which were taken in August and September, and none of which is recorded as having contained embryos. The skulls of the eight August-taken specimens also suggest that young are born in late spring or early summer: the largest skull had well-worn teeth that might indicate an age of more than one year; four others had complete adult dentitions that were barely worn; and three had not yet acquired complete adult dentitions.

The records of E. minimus, like those of Spermophilus lateralis, indicate greatest abundance in the higher parts of the Mesa Verde and in areas of predominantly brushy vegetation.

Eutamias quadrivittatus hopiensis Merriam Colorado Chipmunk

Specimens examined.--Total, 13: Prater Canyon, 7600 ft., MV 7838/507; Lower Well, Prater Canyon, 69278; Park Headquarters, MV 7889/507; near the old Park Well, 7300 ft., 5468 in Univ. of Colorado collection; Utility Area, 5469 and 5470 in Univ. of Colorado collection; Spruce Tree House, 4352-4355 in Denver Museum; Mesa Verde, 25 mi. [by road] SW Mancos, 149080-149081 USNM; Square Tower House, 7000 ft., 5467 in Univ. of Colorado collection.

Although both species occur in some of the same areas, E. q. hopiensis is more abundant than is E. minimus in stands of pinyon and juniper, along cliffs, and at low elevations. (A specimen of hopiensis, MV 7849/507, from 3 mi. S of the Park boundary where the 6000 foot contour line cross the Mancos River is indicative of the occurrence at low elevations.)

Thomomys bottae aureus J.A. Allen Botta's Pocket Gopher

Specimens examined.--Total, 35: Prater Canyon, 7600 ft., 74408-74410 MVZ; Upper Well, Prater Canyon, 7575 ft., 69279; 1/4 mi. N Middle Well, Prater Canyon, 7500 ft., 69280; Middle Well, Prater Canyon, 7500 ft., 69281-69285, 75977; Morfield Canyon, 7600 ft., 75978; 3/4 mi. S, 1-3/4 mi. W Park Point, 8000 ft, 69286-69288; 1-1/4 mi. S, 1-3/4 mi. W Park Point, 8000 ft., 69289; 1-1/2 mi. S, 2 mi. W Park Point, 8075 ft., 69290; Sect. 27, head of east fork Navajo Canyon, 7900 ft, 69291-69292; 1/2 mi. N Far View Ruins, 7825 ft, 69293; Far View Ruins, 7700 ft., 69294, MV 7852/507, 7853/507; 3 mi. N Rock Springs, 8200 ft., 69295-69298; 2-1/2 mi. N, 1/2 mi. W Rock Springs, 8100 ft., 69299-69301; 2 mi. N, 1/4 mi. W Rock Springs, 69302-69303; 1 mi. NNW Rock Springs, 69304; 1/2 mi. NNW Rock Springs, 69305; Mesa Verde, northern end, 8100 ft., 149087 USNM.

The pocket gophers of the Mesa Verde and vicinity are of one species,

Thomomys bottae. The distribution and variation of this species in Colorado have been studied recently by Youngman (1958) who referred all specimens from the Mesa Verde to T. b. aureus. He noted that some specimens have dark diffuse dorsal stripes that are wide in specimens from the Mancos River Valley. The generally darker color of the specimens from the Mancos Valley as compared with that of specimens from on the Mesa was noticed in the field, and is another example of the local variability of pocket gophers. The nine specimens listed by Youngman (1958:372) as from "Mesa Verde National Park," Mancos River, 6200 ft., are not here listed among "specimens examined" because possibly some, or all, of the nine were trapped on the east side of the River and therefore outside the Park. None was, however, farther than 30 yards east of the Park.

In the Park, pocket gophers occur both on mesa tops and in canyons. Most of the localities listed above and others at which mounds were seen are areas of disturbance such as the old burn on Wetherill Mesa, the rights of way for roads, the river valley, and the grazed floor of Prater Canyon. Little evidence of pocket gophers was found on unusually rocky slopes, steep slopes, or in stands of pinyon and juniper or in relatively pure stands of oak-brush. In addition to workability of the soil, the presence of herbaceous plants, many of them weedy annuals, is probably the most important factor governing the success of pocket gophers in a local area. No female was recorded to have contained embryos, but two had enlarged uteri or placental scars. This fact and the capture of nine half-grown individuals indicate breeding prior to late August when most specimens were trapped.

Dipodomys ordii longipes (Merriam) Ord's Kangaroo Rat

Kangaroo rats have been seen crossing the highway in the Park less than one mile from the Park entrance by Jean Pinkley.

Castor canadensis concisor Warren and Hall Beaver

In 1935 Quaintance and White spent June 16 to June 20 in the Mancos River

Bottoms at the mouth of Weber Canyon, looking for sign of fresh beaver work. They found none. Annual Animal Census Reports include the following information based on patrols along the Mancos River at the east boundary of the Park: 1937--estimate 4 beaver present, 1938--8, 1941--numerous bank burrows, 1942--uncommon, 1944--uncommon, 1945--most concentrated at southeast corner, 1946--runs and two small dams seen (flood had washed out larger dams), 1947--only in 1-1/2 miles north of boundary with Ute Reservation, 1949--two separate colonies (each with dams and one with a large house), 1950--none, owing to drouth and diversion of water upstream completely drying the river at times, 1951--none, 1953--present, 1955--present. On the Mancos River, 6200 ft., in late August, 1956, sign of beaver was abundant, numerous trees had been cut but none within a week, and a bank den was found on the west side of the river extending back 50 feet from the stream and caved in at three places. In 1959 dens were still present.

Reithrodontomys megalotis aztecus J.A. Allen Western Harvest Mouse

Specimens examined.--Total, 38: North end Mesa Verde National Park, 7000 ft, 75984-75986; Park Point, 8525 ft., 69316-69317; Far View Ruins, 7700 ft, 69318-69319, 79220, MV 7897/507, and 23 uncatalogued specimens in preservative; 3 mi. N Rock Springs, 8200 ft., 69320-69321; 2 mi. NNW Rock Springs, 7900 ft., 69322-69323; 1 mi. NNW Rock Springs, 7600 ft., 69324; 1/2 mi. NNW Rock Springs, 7500 ft., 69325.

The specimen listed last (69325) was an adult male recovered from the stomach of a small (snout-vent length 334 mm., wt. 26.0 gms.) Crotalus viridis that was trapped in a Museum Special mouse-trap on a rocky slope mostly barren of vegetation. The availability of samples taken in August (by Anderson in 1956), in September (by Shepherd in 1958), and in November (by Alcorn in 1957) makes the following comparison of age and reproductive condition possible. The sample from November includes some specimens from outside the Park as follows: 1 mi. W Mancos, Colorado, 75979-75983, and 2 mi. N La Plata [not shown on Fig. 2], San Juan County, New Mexico, some 18 miles southeast of the Park, 75987-76000. The data shown in Figure 3 indicate that females are pregnant at least from in August into November. A smaller percentage of females was pregnant in November than in August or September. The fact that all females more than 130 mm. long were pregnant in September suggests an autumnal peak in breeding activity. A change in the ratio of small individuals (less than 130 mm. in length) to large individuals (130 mm. or more in length) is indicative of a sustained breeding period throughout the time shown. In August the ratio was 1 to 2.3, in September the ratio was 1 to 1.2, and the ratio was 1 to 0.7 in November. The western harvest mouse is found usually in grassy areas.

Peromyscus boylii rowleyi (J.A. Allen) Brush Mouse

Specimens examined.--Total, 14: North end Mesa Verde National Park, 7000 ft., 76002-76003; Far View House, 7700 ft., MV 7851/507, 7854/507; Far View Point, 5 uncatalogued specimens in preservative; 1/2 mi. N Spruce Tree Lodge, 34742; 25 mi. [by road] SW Mancos, 149094 and 149096 USNM; Oak Tree Ruin, 6700 ft., MV 7870/507; and Cliff Palace, 6800 ft., MV 7864/507.

The specimens were taken in August, September, and November. One adult female trapped on September 10, 1958, had six embryos.

Peromyscus crinitus auripectus (J.A. Allen) Canyon Mouse

Specimens examined.--Total, 3: Mesa Verde [Spruce Tree Cliff Ruins], 149095 USNM; Balcony House, MV 7865/507, 7866/507.

Peromyscus maniculatus rufinus (Merriam) Deer Mouse

Specimens examined.--Total, 396: North end Mesa Verde National Park, 7000 ft., 76004-76100; Prater Canyon, 7600 ft., 76101-76144, MV 7839/507, 7840/507; Upper Well, Prater Canyon, 7575 ft., 69328-69329; Morfield Canyon, 7600 ft., 76145-76184; Park Point, 8525 ft., 69330-69342, 69344-69360; 1-1/2 mi. E Waters Cabin, 6400 ft. (labels on some specimens read "West Bank Mancos River, Northeast side Mesa Verde National Park"),

69361-69376, 76185-76204; Sect. 27, head of east fork Navajo Canyon, 7900 ft., 69377-69380, 69422-69426; 3 mi. N Rock Springs, 8200 ft., 69403-69410; 2 mi. NNW Rock Springs, 7900 ft., 69411-69412; 1 mi. NNW Rock Springs, 7600 ft., 69413-69418; 1/2 mi. NNW Rock Springs, 7500 ft., 69419-69421; Far View Ruins, 7700 ft., 69386-69402; Far View Point, 76530-76531, 79221 and 90 uncatalogued specimens in preservative; Mancos River, 6200 ft., 69382-69385; back of Park Museum, 6930 ft., MV 7857/507; Mesa Verde, 25 mi. [by road] SW Mancos, 149093 USNM; Cornfield, MV 7878/507.

The most abundant mammal is the ubiquitous deer mouse. Series of specimens taken in August (by Anderson in 1956), in September (by Shepherd in 1958 and 1959), and in November (by Alcorn in 1957) make possible the following comparisons of age, reproductive conditions, and molts.

The specimens obtained in August and November were placed in five categories according to age (as judged by wear on the teeth). These categories correspond in general to those used by Hoffmeister (1951:1) in studies of Peromyscus truei. From his descriptions I judge that wear in Peromyscus maniculatus differs from wear in Peromyscus truei in that the last upper molar is not worn smooth before appreciable wear appears on the first two molars, and the lingual and labial cusps wear more nearly concurrently. The five categories differ as follows: category 1, last upper molar in process of erupting, showing no wear; category 2, some wear apparent on all teeth, but most cusps little worn; category 3, greater wear on all teeth, lingual cusps becoming rounded or flattened; category 4, lingual cusps worn smooth, labial cusps show considerable wear; category 5, all cusps worn smooth. The condition of the pelage was noted for each prepared skin. Hoffmeister (op. cit.: 4) summarized changes in pelage that he observed in Peromyscus truei, and he summarized earlier work by Collins with Peromyscus maniculatus. In P. maniculatus a grayish juvenal pelage is replaced by a postjuvenal pelage in which the hairs are longer and have longer, pale, terminal or subterminal bands giving a paler and more buffy or ochraceous hue to the dorsal pelage. The postjuvenal pelage is replaced by an adult pelage that is either brighter or, in some cases, is not distinguishable with certainty from the postjuvenal pelage. Not only is the juvenal pelage distinguishable from the postjuvenal pelage, but the sequence of ingrowth of postjuvenal pelage follows a regular pattern that is usually different from that of subsequent molts. The loss of juvenal hair is less readily observed than the ingrowth of new postjuvenal hair on account of the greater time required for the growth of any individual hair than for the sudden loss of a hair.

Molt was observed in some individuals no longer having juvenal pelage; some new pelage was observed on the skins of seven mice collected in August. Each of these was in category 4 or 5 and probably had been born in the previous calendar year. These seven molting individuals make up nearly 17 per cent of 42 individuals that had completed the juvenal to postjuvenal molt. In November, 80 per cent of individuals (92 of 115) that had previously obtained their postjuvenal or adult pelage were molting. These mice were in age-categories 3, 4, and 5. Some of the individuals in category 3 were developing new hair beneath a relatively unworn bright pelage that I judge to be an adult pelage rather than a postjuvenal pelage. If this judgment be correct and if the relatively unworn dentition (category 3) means that these animals are young of the year, we must conclude that individuals born in early summer may molt from juvenal to postjuvenal, then to adult pelage, and finally in the autumn into another adult pelage. Other individuals, six in number and of categories 2 and 3, are simultaneously completing the juvenal to postjuvenal molt and beginning the postjuvenal to adult molt. The juvenal to postjuvenal molt begins, as has been described by various authors, along the lateral line and proceeds dorsally and ventrally and anteriorly and posteriorly, and the last patch to lose the gray juvenal color is the top of head and nape, or less frequently the rump. In some individuals a gray patch on the nape remained but emerging hair was not apparent; perhaps the molt had been halted just prior to completion. The progressing band of emerging hair is narrow in most specimens but in some up to one-fifth of the circumference of the body has hair at the same degree of emergence. Subsequent molts, both from postjuvenal to adult pelage and between adult pelages, are less regular in point, or points, of origin, width of progressing molt, and amount of surface molting at one time. Half or more of the dorsum is oftentimes involved in the same stage of molt at once. In some specimens the molt begins along the lateral line, and in others in several centers on the sides. In some skins distinct lines of molt are visible without parting the hair, and in some others the molt is patchy in appearance. Growth of new hair is apparent at various times of the year as a result of injury such as that caused by bot fly larvae, cuts, scratches, or bites of other mice. Abrasion, wear, irritation by ectoparasites, and other kinds of injury to the skin may play a part in the development of a patchy molt. Both breeding and molting are sources of considerable stress, and the delay of the peak of molting activity until November when breeding activity has decreased seems of benefit to the mice. A change in the ratio of young mice (categories 1, 2, and 3) to old mice (categories 4 and 5) between August and November was noted. In August, 29 per cent of the population is composed of old mice, and in November only 6 per cent. This change results from birth of young as well as death of old mice, but may indicate that a mouse in November has less than one chance in ten of being alive the following November. Some females born early in the reproductive season breed in their first summer or autumn. For example, a female of category 2, taken on August 12, and probably in postjuvenal pelage, had placental scars. Undoubtedly the young of the year contribute to the breeding population, especially late in the season.

In Figure 3 the proportion of females bearing embryos in August, September, and November is shown. Of the females trapped in August, 11 of 32 that were more than 144 mm. in total length contained embryos; an additional 14 females were lactating or possessed placental scars or enlarged uteri. Therefore, approximately 80 per cent of the larger females were reproducing in August. In September two females were pregnant and an additional sixteen of the 44 females examined showed other evidence of reproduction; these eighteen females make up 41 per cent of those more than 144 mm. in total length. The only reproductive data available for November pertain to the presence or absence of embryos. No female was pregnant although 35 females more than 144 mm. in total length were examined. Some of the skins show prominent mammae indicative of recent nursing, and juveniles less than a month old were taken. The reproductive activity of deer mice on the Mesa Verde seems to be greatly reduced in autumn.

Peromyscus difficilis nasutus (J.A. Allen) Rock Mouse

Specimen: 1 mi. NNW Rock Springs, 7600 ft., 69413, a young individual completing the molt from juvenal to postjuvenal pelage.

Peromyscus truei truei (Shufeldt) Pinyon Mouse

Specimens examined.--Total, 42: North end Mesa Verde National Park, 7000 ft., 76220-76232; Far View Ruins, 7700 ft., 69326-69327, 79222, and 8 uncatalogued specimens in preservative; Far View Point, 76532-76535; Far View House, 7700 ft., 74416 MVZ; 1/2 mi. NNW Rock Springs, 7500 ft., 69429-69430; Rock Springs, 7400 ft., 69431-69435; Park Well, 7450 ft., 69428; Headquarters, MV 7882/507; back of Museum, MV 7879/507, 7880/507, 7881/507; Square Tower House, 6700 ft., 69438.

In August three females were pregnant or lactating, or both. None of seven adult females taken in November was pregnant.

Neotoma cinerea arizonae Merriam Bushy-tailed Wood Rat

Specimen: Head of Prater Canyon, MV 7873/507. Another, in the Denver Museum, from Spruce Tree House, was reported by Finley (1958:270).

Neotoma cinerea prefers vertical crevices in high cliffs but occupies other areas.

Neotoma mexicana inopinata Goldman Mexican Wood Rat

Specimens examined.--Total, 10: Headquarters, MV 7890/507 and probably 7861/507, 74421 MVZ; Spruce Tree Lodge, 6950 ft., 34802-34803; Spruce Tree House, 74419-74420 MVZ; Square Tower House, MV 7869/507; Cliff Palace, 74422 MVZ; Balcony House, MV 7868/507.

The Mexican wood rat is the most common species of wood rat on the Mesa Verde. The two specimens from Spruce Tree Lodge obtained by R.B. Finley on September 2, 1949, are young individuals.

Another species of the genus, the white-throated wood rat, Neotoma albigula, may occur within the Park, since three specimens (34757-34759) from the Mesa Verde were trapped on September 15, 1949, by R.B. Finley, approximately 4-1/2 miles south of the Park [6 mi. E, 17 mi. S Cortez, 5600 ft.--south of the area shown in Figure 2]. Finley (1958:450) stated that at that locality he trapped Neotoma mexicana [No. 34801], that N. albigula was perhaps more common there than N. mexicana, that dens of N. albigula were more common than those of N. mexicana under large rocks in the talus on the south slope of the Mesa, and that dens of N. mexicana seemed to be more numerous in crevices of ledges in the bedrock and cliffs.

Ondatra zibethicus osoyoosensis (Lord) Muskrat

D. Watson (in letter of January 16, 1957) reported that he has seen muskrat tracks many times along the Mancos River. He also relates a report received from Chief Ranger Wade and D.A. Spencer who saw a muskrat, no doubt a wanderer, on the Knife Edge Road on a cold winter night. These men, both reliable observers, stopped and saw the muskrat at a distance of two feet, where it took shelter under a power shovel parked beside the road. Reports of dens seen along the Mancos River are available for 1944, 1945, 1946, and 1947.

Microtus longicaudus mordax (Merriam) Long-tailed Vole

Specimens examined.--Total, 36: North end Mesa Verde National Park, 7000 ft., 76233-76237; entrance to Mesa Verde National Park, 5123-5126 in Denver Museum; Prater Canyon, 7600 ft., 76238-76244; Upper Well, Prater Canyon, 7575 ft., 69441; Morfield Canyon, 7600 ft., 76245-76259, 76261-76263; west bank Mancos River, northeast side Mesa Verde National Park, 76260.

The vegetation at the above-named localities is a combination of brush and grasses that are both more luxuriant than in areas dominated by pinyon and juniper on the more southern and altitudinally lower part of the top of the Mesa where no M. longicaudus was taken.

Microtus mexicanus mogollonensis (Mearns) Mexican Vole

Specimens examined.--Total, 22: Prater Canyon, 7600 ft., 76283-76287; Sect. 27, head of east fork of Navajo Canyon, 7900 ft., 69442; Far View Ruins, 7700 ft., 69443, 79223-79224; 2 mi. NNW Rock Springs, 7900 ft., 69444-69446; Park Well, 7450 ft., 69447-69453; rock ledge at head of Spruce Tree Canyon, unnumbered specimen in Denver Museum; Headquarters, MV 7895/507, 7896/507.

The first specimen of the Mexican vole from Colorado was obtained on the Mesa Verde and has been reported by Rodeck and Anderson (1956:436). Specimens have now been taken at seven localities on the Mesa. Prater Canyon is the only one of these localities at which any other species of vole was taken. There Microtus longicaudus and Microtus montanus were also obtained. Judging from the vegetation at the above localities, M. mexicanus is to be expected in drier areas with less cover than M. montanus inhabits, and in areas having less cover than those inhabited by M. longicaudus.

Microtus montanus fusus Hall Montane Vole

Specimens examined.--Total, 16: Upper Well, 7575 ft., 69454-69465; 1/4 mi. N Middle Well, 7500 ft., 69466-69469.

The voles were trapped in the dry but dense meadow of grass and sedge covering the floor of the canyon (see Plate 1). Sorex vagrans was trapped in the same places. Four of the females of M. montanus trapped on September 3, 1956, were pregnant.

Erethizon dorsatum couesi Mearns Porcupine

Specimens examined.--Total, 2: 69470, old [Female], and 69471, her young male offspring, both obtained on August 28, 1956, in the canyon of the Mancos River, 6200 feet, along the western side of the River.

I saw no other porcupine in the Park.

In 1935, C.W. Quaintance took special notice of porcupines because of the possibility, then being considered, of their being detrimental to habitat conditions thought to be favorable to wild turkeys. Porcupines were suspected of killing ponderosa pine, which occurred in only a few places, and which was thought to be necessary for wild turkeys. Porcupines were recorded as follows: one found dead on the road at the North Rim on March 16; one killed in oak brush along the North Rim; one killed between April 15 and May 15; oak brush damaged by porcupines in Soda Canyon below the well; one seen on July 4 on the Poole Canyon Trail; one seen at the foot of the Mesa on June 26; one seen by Lloyd White in Moccasin Canyon on June 27; and one seen by Mrs. Sharon Spencer on July 1 in Prater Canyon. After four months on the Mesa Verde, Quaintance concluded that there were not so many porcupines as had been expected and that there were more ponderosa pines than had been expected.

In 1946, Donald A. Spencer began a study of porcupines on the Mesa Verde and in 1958 deposited, in the University of Colorado Library, his results in manuscript form as a dissertation in partial fulfillment of the requirements for a higher degree ("Porcupine population fluctuations in past centuries revealed by dendrochronology," 108 numbered and 13 unnumbered pages, 39 figures, and 13 tables). Dendrochronology, or the dating of trees by studying their rings, is a technique widely used in the southwest by archeologists, climatologists, and others. Spencer found that porcupines damage trees in a characteristic manner, and that damage to a pinyon pine was evident as long as the tree lived. By dating approximately 2000 scars and plotting the year for each scar, Spencer observed three peaks since 1865; these were in about 1885, 1905, and 1935. The increase and decrease each time were at about the same rate. The study did not yield precise population estimates. Some porcupines were destroyed but Spencer is of the opinion that the decline that came in following years was independent of the control measures. Spencer thinks that activities of porcupines on the Mesa Verde are a major factor in maintaining a forest cover of relatively young trees, and also in preventing invasion of trees into areas of brush.

The general policy in regard to porcupines from 1930 to 1946 was to kill them because they eat parts of trees. In at least the following years porcupines were killed: 1930, 1933, 1935, 1940, 1943, 1944, and 1946. The largest number reported killed in one year is 71 in 1933 when a crew of men was employed for this purpose. The amount of effort devoted to killing porcupines varied from year to year. The most frequently voiced alarm was that the scenic value of the areas along the entrance highway and near certain ruins was being impaired. The direst prediction was that all pine trees on the Mesa Verde were doomed to extinction in the near future. The last prediction has not come to pass, nor has this extinction occurred in the past thousand years and more during which pine trees and porcupines have existed together on the Mesa Verde.

In 1946 the studies of Spencer, Wade, and Fitch began. Much effort was expended in obtaining and dating scars for analysis, and the interesting results mentioned above were the reward. Also many porcupines were captured alive and marked with ear-tags so that they could be recognized later. For example, in the winter of 1946 and 1947, 117 were marked in Soda Canyon. A decline in numbers in recent years reduced the impetus for continuation of the study by reducing the results obtained for each day spent searching for porcupines. Information obtained on movements of porcupines relative to season and weather conditions in these studies may be summarized and published later. Data regarding ratio of young to adult animals from year to year are also of interest.

The effect of a porcupine on a single tree is often easy to assess. The effect of a fluctuating population of porcupines on a mixed forest is not so easy to assess, but is of more intrinsic interest. It is desirable that studies designed to evaluate the latter effect continue while the population remains low and also when the next cyclic increase begins. Publication of Spencer's results would be a major step forward.

Cahalane (1948:253) mentions the difficulty that has been experienced in protecting aesthetically desirable trees around cliff dwellings. Perhaps in a local area removal of porcupines is sometimes warranted, but control of the porcupine seems undesirable to me, as a general policy, because one purpose of a National Park is to preserve natural conditions and that implies naturally occurring changes.

What is needed is continued careful study of the ecological relationships of animals and of plants. National parks provide, to the extent that they are not disturbed or "controlled," especially favorable places for studies of this sort.

Mus musculus subsp. House Mouse

Specimens examined.--Total, 7: North end Mesa Verde National Park, 7000 ft, 76290; west bank Mancos River northeast side Mesa Verde National Park, 76291-76296.

Canis latrans mearnsi Merriam Coyote

Specimens examined.--Total, 3: 69472, skull only of a young individual, found dead at the top of the bank of the Mancos River, 1-1/2 mi. E Waters Cabin, 6400 ft., August 29, 1956, probably killed by man; ad. [Male], 76298, taken by J.R. Alcorn, November 10, 1957, on the top of the Mesa at Square Tower House; and skin and skull, MV 7858/507, without data.

Tracks or scats of the coyote were seen in all parts of the Park visited. Coyotes range throughout the area. On September 3, 1956, 35 coyote scats were found on the dirt roads in Prater and Morfield canyons above 7300 feet elevation and on the road crossing the divide between these canyons. Probably none of these scats was more than a month old. Coyote tracks were seen at some of the fresher scats. Scats associated with fox tracks and scats of small size were not picked up. Nevertheless, a few of the scats studied may have been those of foxes. Judging from the contents of scats that were certainly from foxes, the effect of inadvertent inclusion of fox scats would be to elevate the percentage of scats containing berries (but not more than five percentage points). Each scat was broken up and the percentage of scats containing each of the following items was noted (figures are to the nearest per cent). Remains of deer occurred in 48 per cent of scats, gooseberries (Ribes) in 34 per cent, porcupines in 29 per cent, insects in 11 per cent, birds in 11 per cent, unidentified hair in 9 per cent, and unidentified material in 6 per cent. One scat (3 per cent) contained an appreciable amount of plant debris, one contained Microtus along with other items, and one contained only Sylvilagus; 14 scats had material of more than one category. The percentage in each category of the volume of each scat was estimated. Data on volume warrant no conclusion other than one that can be drawn from the percentages of occurrence, namely that the major food sources used in August, 1956, by coyotes in these canyons were deer, berries, and porcupines and that other sources, though used, were relatively unimportant. Deer were common in the area. It is fortunate that coyotes remain to help regulate the deer population. Wolves, Canis lupus, which at one time occurred in the Park, are now gone. The coyote and mountain lion are the only sizeable predators that remain.

Vulpes vulpes macroura Baird Red Fox

D. Watson (in letter of January 16, 1957) reported that red foxes have been seen on the Mesa by several employees of the Park. These persons know the gray fox, which often is seen in winter feeding at their back doors, and Mr. Watson considers the reports reliable. In the early morning of October 24, 1943, a reddish-yellow fox having a white-tipped tail was observed by three men, one of whom was Chief Ranger Wade, at Park Point. In 1948, 1950, and 1953 black foxes have been reported.

Urocyon cinereoargenteus scottii Mearns Gray Fox

Specimens examined.--Total, 3: [Male], MV 7867/507, 2 mi. N of Headquarters, 7400 ft., September 24, 1935, H.P. Pratt; [Male], 76299, November 9, and [Female], 76300, trapped on November 12, 1957, by J.R. Alcorn at Square Tower House.

The gray fox is common on the Mesa.

Ursus americanus amblyceps Baird Black Bear

From 1929 through 1959 at least 151 observations of bears were recorded. Observations were unrecorded in only five years--1952, 1953, 1954, 1956, and 1958. Most observations were in the 1940's and the peak was in 1944 (18 observations) and 1945 (21 observations). Cubs have been recorded in 10 different years. If dated reports are tabulated by months the following figures are obtained for the 12 months beginning with January: 0, 0, 0, 4, 15, 19, 19, 9, 10, 9, 3, 0. The peak in the summer months and the absence of observations in the winter months are significant. Individual bears probably enter and leave the Park in the course of their normal wanderings; however bears probably hibernate, breed, and bear young within the Park and should not be regarded as merely occasionally wandering into the Park.

Procyon lotor pallidus Merriam Raccoon

In December, 1959, three raccoons were seen on Prater Grade and later three were seen in Morfield Canyon near the tunnel. I saw a dead raccoon at the side of the highway 3 mi. WSW of Mancos, 6700 feet, on August 8, 1956. This locality is outside of the Park and not on the Mesa, but is mentioned because it indicates that the raccoon probably occurs along the Mancos River, which forms the eastern boundary of the Park. The raccoon is rare in the area. Some local persons were surprised to hear of its presence; other persons told me that raccoons were present, but rare.

Bassariscus astutus flavus Rhoads Ringtail

Specimens examined.--Total, 4: MV 7884/507 and 7885/507, trapped in Balcony House and prepared by D. Watson in 1939; MV 7901/507 and 7902/507, without data.

The cliff dwellings are favored by ringtails and in some years they are common near occupied dwellings in the area of headquarters. Ringtails have been seen in each major habitat within the Park.

Mustela frenata nevadensis Hall Long-tailed Weasel

Specimens examined.--Total, 5: MV 7891/507, [Male], from the "Garden" [= Indian Cornfield]; [Female], MV 7892/507, also from the "Cornfield"; MV 7859/507, "Killed by car on Prater Grade"; [Male], MV 7871/507, in winter pelage, from the North Rim; and [Male], 83464, killed on the road 1/2 mi. NE of the tunnel, Morfield Canyon.

C.W. Quaintance in 1935 reported that on January 11, he and Mr. Nelson saw a weasel attack a cottontail, and on March 9, while on the snow plow, Mr. Nelson witnessed another cottontail being killed by a weasel. Weasels in white winter pelage have been recorded in December and January. The brown pelage has been seen as late as November.

Mustela vison energumenos (Bangs) Mink

D. Watson (in letter of January 16, 1957) wrote: "When Jack Wade, now Chief Ranger, was doing patrol work in the Mancos Canyon back in the 1930's, he saw mink along the river at the east side of the Park. Several years ago, the people who lived on the ranch where Weber Canyon joins the Mancos trapped a mink." Tracks have been reported along the Mancos River in several years.

Spilogale putorius gracilis Merriam Spotted Skunk

Specimen: Immature [Male], MV 7860/507, Cliff Palace, August 22, 1936, prepared by A.E. Borrell.

In some years these little skunks have become so numerous in the area of headquarters that they were a nuisance, and were captured in garbage cans and released in other parts of the Park.

Mephitis mephitis estor Merriam Striped Skunk

D. Watson advises me that striped skunks are fairly common around the entrance to the Park, along the foot of the Mesa, and along the Mancos River. Striped skunks have been reported in 1951 in Morfield Canyon, in 1952 on the Knife Edge, in 1953 at Windy Point (1/4 mi. N of Point Lookout), and in 1959 at the head of Morfield Canyon.

UPPER: View of the North Rim of Mesa Verde, looking west from Park Point, the highest place on the North Rim. The south-facing slope on the left is covered with brushy vegetation, mostly oak. Sheltered parts of the north-facing slope support stands of Douglas fir, and at a few places some ponderosa pines. Photo taken in August, 1956, by S. Anderson.

LOWER LEFT: View of Rock Canyon from Wetherill Mesa, looking southwest from a point 2 mi. NNW Rock Springs. The area in the foreground on Wetherill Mesa was burned in 1934. Photo taken in August, 1956, by S. Anderson.

LOWER RIGHT: Prater Canyon, at Upper Well, 7575 feet. In the matted grasses and sedges on the floor of the canyon Microtus montanus and Sorex vagrans were captured. Tamiasciurus hudsonicus was found in a side canyon, Chickaree Draw, one half mile southwest of the place shown. Chickaree Draw is more sheltered than the slope in the background and has a denser stand of Douglas fir than occurs here. Photo taken in August, 1956, by S. Anderson.]

UPPER: Relatively undisturbed stand of pinyon pine and Utah juniper 1/4 mi. N Rock Springs, at 7400 feet elevation on Wetherill Mesa along a service road.

The vegetation shown is characteristic of the lower more exposed parts of the top of the Mesa Verde. Photo taken in August, 1956, by S. Anderson.

LOWER: Wetherill Mesa, 1/2 mi. NNW Rock Springs, 7500 feet elevation. This area burned in 1934. It contained no pine or juniper in 1956 despite attempted reforestation in the thirties and the presence of a stand of pinyon and juniper (shown above) only one quarter of a mile away. Possibly fire in the last three or four hundred years on the higher parts of the Mesa has been a factor in producing chaparral there, rather than pinyon and juniper. Photo taken in August, 1956, by S. Anderson.]

Taxidea taxus berlandieri Baird Badger

Several reports, but no specimens, of the badger have been obtained. In 1935, C.W. Quaintance wrote that in School Section Canyon tracks of cougar, bobcat, coyote, and deer were found, and that pocket gophers, badgers, and cottontail rabbits were present. Later in 1935, H.P. Pratt wrote that he had found evidence of badgers "at the lower well in Prater Canyon, where on September 23, there were extensive badger diggings and fresh tracks in the vicinity of the prairie dog colony there." Badgers are common in the lowlands around the Mesa and they are common enough on the Mesa to be regarded as nuisances by archeologists on account of badgers digging in ruins. Badgers have been seen from three to six times each year from 1950 to this date, most of them in the vicinity of the North Rim.

Felis concolor hippolestes Merriam Mountain Lion

Mountain lions range throughout the Park. There are reliable sight records of lions and lion tracks, but no specimen has been preserved. Early records of observations include the report of tracks seen in Navajo Canyon by Cary (1911:165), and a lion seen in 1917. Since 1930 the more adequate records include reports of from one to eight observations each year for 26 of the 30 years. Young animals (recorded as "half-grown") or cubs have been reported in four of these years. The tabulation of dated reports by month beginning with

January is: 2, 0, 3, 2, 8, 4, 6, 7, 4, 9, 5, 7. Mountain lions range more widely than bears in their daily and seasonal activities, but like bears probably breed, bear young, and feed in the Park. Although at any one time lions may or may not be within the Park, it is part of their normal range and the species should be regarded as resident and is not uncommon.

Lynx rufus baileyi Merriam Bobcat

Specimens examined.--Total, 2: A specimen (now mounted in Park Museum) from the Knife Edge Road; and ad. [Female], 76302, Prater Canyon, 7500 ft., November 12, 1957, obtained by J.R. Alcorn.

Bobcats are present throughout the Park. Approximately 80 observations of bobcats are on file, from all parts of the Park and in all months. Probably the bobcat and the gray fox are the most abundant carnivores in the Park. In addition to known predation by mountain lions and coyotes on porcupines, the bobcat kills porcupines. A dead porcupine and a dead bobcat with its face, mouth, and one foot full of quills were found together on January 31, 1952, under a boulder in front of Cliff Palace. On August 20, 1956, I saw a bobcat hunting in sage in a draw near a large clump of oak-brush, into which it fled, at the head of the east fork of Navajo Canyon, Sect. 21, near the North Rim, 8100 feet.

Odocoileus hemionus hemionus (Rafinesque) Mule Deer

Specimens examined.--Total, 2: Young [Male], 76303, November 8, 1957, Far View Ruins; [Female], 76304, November 12, 1957, Spruce Tree House Ruin, both obtained by J.R. Alcorn.

In all parts of the Park, mule deer are common. Five projects concerning deer are in progress or have been concluded recently on the Mesa. One is a study of the responses of different species of plants to browsing and was begun in 1949 by Harold R. Shepherd for the Colorado Department of Game and Fish. A number of individual plants and in some instances groups of plants were fenced to exclude deer. Systematic clips of 20, 40, 60, 80, or 100 per cent of the annual growth are made each year. The results of the first ten years of this study are being prepared for publication by Shepherd.

A study of browsing pressure was initiated in 1952 by Regional Biologist C.M. Aldous, on eight transects in the Park. Each transect consists of 15 plots at intervals of 200 feet. The amount of use of each plant species was recorded from time to time. The study was terminated in 1955. I have seen no summary of results of this study.

A trapping program was begun in 1953 with the co-operation of the Colorado Department of Game and Fish. Deer are trapped, marked, and released. Some are released in areas other than where trapped. In this way the excessive size of the herd near headquarters has been reduced. Recoveries of marked deer outside the Park by hunters and retrapping results in the Park should provide information about movements of deer and about life expectancy.

The "Deer Trend Study" was initiated in 1954. From November to May, twice a day, at the same time, a count is made along the entrance road from the Park Entrance to Headquarters. Ten drainage areas traversed are tabulated separately. The results of four years of this study indicate that the greatest number of deer are present in November, December, and January, and that only about one-fourth as many are present in February and March. Depending on severity of weather, the yearly pattern varies, the deer arriving earlier, or leaving earlier. This change in numbers, the recovery outside of the Park of animals marked in the Park, and direct observations of movement indicate that the Mesa Verde is an intermediate range rather than a summer-range or winter-range. In summer deer tend to move northward and eastward out of the Park, and in winter they move back through the Park toward lower and more protected areas in canyons both in the Park and south of the Park on the Ute Reservation. Some deer remain in the Park the entire year. Close co-operation between personnel of the Park Service and of the Colorado Department of Game and Fish has regulated hunting outside the Park in such a way as to provide satisfactory control of the deer within the Park.

A study of the effect of rodents on plants used by deer was initiated in 1956 by Harold R. Shepherd. Three acres were fenced in a fashion designed to exclude rodents but not deer. An adjacent three acres were fenced as a control, but not so as to exclude rodents or deer. Eight trap lines nearby provide an index of rodent fluctuations from year to year. These studies will need to be continued for a period of ten years or more, and should provide much information concerning not only deer but also rodents and their effect on vegetation.

Cervus canadensis nelsoni V. Bailey Wapiti

Wapiti are seen periodically; probably they wander in from the higher mountains to the northeast and do not remain for long. The following note was included in the 1921 report of Mr. Jesse L. Nusbaum, then Superintendent of the Park: "The first elk ever seen in the Park made his appearance near the head of Navajo Canyon, August 15 of this year, and travelled for two miles in front of a Ford car down the main road before another car, travelling in the opposite direction, scared him into the timber." Additional observations have been recorded as follows: School Section Canyon ("fall" 1935), Knife Edge Road (July, 1940), West Soda Canyon and Windy Point (December, 1949), Long Canyon (July, 1959), and Park Entrance (December, 1959). Three of the six observations are in July and August; therefore movement by wapiti into the Park can not be attributed entirely to disturbance during the hunting season.

Ovis canadensis canadensis Shaw Bighorn

Some early records of the bighorn were mentioned by C.W. Quaintance (1935): In a letter of January 20, 1935, John Wetherill said that a "Mountain Sheep Canyon" (now Rock Canyon) was named for a bunch of sheep that wintered near their camp; and Sam Ahkeah, a Navajo, says the Indians occasionally find remnants of sheep on the Mesa, which they take back to their hogans. Cahalane (1948:257) reported that hunting presumably had eliminated bighorns from the Mesa by 1896; however Jean Pinkley reports that a large ram was killed on Point Lookout in 1906.

On January 30, 1946, 14 sheep (3 rams, 7 ewes, and 4 lambs) from the herd at Tarryall, Colorado, were obtained through the Colorado Department of Game and Fish and were released at 8:30 a.m. at the edge of the canyon south of Spruce Tree Lodge. The sheep, instead of entering the canyon as expected, turned north, passed behind the museum, and eventually disappeared northward on Chapin Mesa. The sheep evidently divided into at least two bands. On April 24, 1946, three sheep were seen 2-1/2 mi. N of Rock Springs, and on June 19, 1947, tracks were seen in Mancos Canyon. In 1947, 1948, and 1949 farmers in Weber Canyon reported seeing sheep many times on Weber Mountain, and watering at the Mancos River. In May, 1949, an estimate of 27 sheep on Weber Mountain was made after several days study by men from the state game department. The herds continued to increase. In 1956 I saw two bighorns. On August 18, at 6:20 a.m., my wife and I briefly observed a bighorn on the rocks below Square Tower Ruins. On August 24, I was digging with a small shovel in rocky soil behind the cabin at Rock Springs, when hoof beats were heard approaching in the rocky head of the canyon to the east. An adult ewe came up to the fence around the cabin area and looked at me, seemingly curious about the noise my shovel had been producing. I remained motionless and called to my wife, Justine, to come from the cabin and see the sheep. The ewe seemed not to be disturbed by my voice, but took flight, returning in the direction from which she had come, the moment Justine appeared from behind the cabin. Sheep can now be seen on occasion in any of the deep canyons across the southern half of the Park. The sheep have caused slight damage in some of the ruins by bedding down there, and by climbing on walls. As the sheep increase in numbers this activity may be regarded as a problem. In 1959 an estimated 75 to 100 sheep were in the Park and adjacent areas.

DISCUSSION

The distributions of animals are influenced by geographic, vegetational, and altitudinal factors. The Mesa Verde is intermediate in geographic position and altitude between the high Southern Rocky Mountains and the low southwestern desert. For this reason, we find on the Mesa Verde (1) a preponderance of species having wide distributions in this part of the country, and having relatively wide ranges of tolerance for different habitats, (2) a lesser number of exclusively montane or boreal species than occur in the higher mountains to the northeast of the Mesa and that may reach the limits of their ranges here, and (3) a small number of species of southern or Sonoran affinities. Fifty-four species are recorded above.

Forty-one of these species are represented by specimens from the Park. Thirteen additional species in the list have been seen in the Park.

On the Grand Mesa, which is more elevated than, and some 110 miles north of, the Mesa Verde (see Figure 1), 55 per cent of the species of mammals have boreal affinities and the other 45 per cent are wide-spread species (Anderson, 1959:414). Boreal species from the Mesa Verde are Sorex vagrans, Sylvilagus nuttallii, Spermophilus lateralis, Marmota flaviventris, Tamiasciurus hudsonicus, Microtus montanus, and Microtus longicaudus. These seven species comprise only thirteen per cent of the mammalian fauna of the Mesa Verde. Other boreal species that occur in the mountains of Colorado on the Grand Mesa or elsewhere (Findley and Anderson, 1956:80) and that do not occur on the Mesa Verde are Sorex cinereus, Sorex palustris, Ochotona princeps, Lepus americana, Clethrionomys gapperi, Phenacomys intermedius, Zapus princeps, Martes americana, Mustela erminea, and Lynx canadensis. The 47 species from the Mesa Verde that are not exclusively boreal make up 87 per cent of the mammalian fauna. Most of these are wide-spread species and are more abundant in the deserts or other lowlands than in the coniferous forests of the highlands, for example the eight species of bats, and Sylvilagus audubonii, Thomomys bottae, Taxidea taxus, Bassariscus astutus, Canis latrans, Cynomys gunnisoni, Reithrodontomys megalotis, and Lepus californicus. A few of the wide-spread species are more common in the highlands than in the lowlands, for example Ursus americanus, Felis concolor, Castor canadensis, Erethizon dorsatum, and Cervus canadensis, and the ranges of three of these, the bear, mountain lion and wapiti, are more restricted today than formerly. A few species find their favorite habitat and reach their greatest abundance in altitudinally and vegetationally intermediate areas such as upon the Mesa Verde, or in special habitats, such as the rock ledges, and crevices that are so abundant on the Mesa. Examples of this group of species are Spermophilus variegatus, Peromyscus crinitus, Peromyscus truei, Neotoma cinerea, and Neotoma mexicana. One species, Dipodomys ordii, is restricted to the desert. Species that are restricted to the desert and that occur in Montezuma County, Colorado, but that are not known from the Mesa Verde are Ammospermophilus leucurus, Perognathus flavus, and Onychomys leucogaster.

Species known to have changed in numbers in the past 50 years are the mule deer that has increased, and the prairie dog that has decreased. Possibly beaver have increased along the Mancos River. The muskrat, mink, beaver, and raccoon usually occur only along the Mancos River, as there is no other permanent surface water in the Park.

Species such as the bighorn and the marmot that are rare within the Park, or those such as the chickaree, the prairie dog, the wandering shrew, the montane vole, and the long-tailed vole that occupy only small areas of suitable habitat within the Park are the species most likely to be eliminated by natural changes, or through the activities of man. For example parasites introduced through domestic sheep that wander into the range of bighorns within the Park might endanger the bighorn population. An increase in grazing activity, road building, and camping in Prater and Morfield canyons might eliminate the small areas of habitat occupied by the montane vole and the wandering shrew. Fire in Chickaree Draw could destroy all the Douglas fir there, and consequently much of the habitat occupied by the chickaree.

Probably some species inhabit the Mesa that have not yet been found, but they are probably few, and their discovery will not alter the faunal pattern in which the few boreal species occupy restricted habitats in the higher parts of the Mesa, and a preponderance of geographically wide-spread species occupy all or most of the Mesa, and surrounding areas. Additional bats are the species most likely to be added to the list.

28-7577

LITERATURE CITED

ANDERSON, S. 1959. Mammals of the Grand Mesa, Colorado. Univ. Kansas Publ., Mus. Nat. Hist, 9(16):405-414, 1 fig. in text.

CAHALANE, V.H. 1948. The status of mammals in the U.S. National Park System, 1947. Jour. Mamm., 29(3):247-259.

CARY, M. 1911. A biological survey of Colorado. N. Amer. Fauna, 33:1-256, 39 figs., frontispiece (map).

FINDLEY, J.S. 1955. Speciation of the Wandering Shrew. Univ. Kansas Publ., Mus. Nat. Hist., 9(1):1-68, figs. 1-18.

FINDLEY, J.S. and ANDERSON, S. 1956. Zoogeography of the montane mammals of Colorado. Jour. Mamm., 37(1):80-82,1 fig. in text.

FINLEY, R.B. 1958. The wood rats of Colorado, distribution and ecology. Univ. Kansas Publ., Mus. Nat. Hist., 10(6):213-552, 34 plates, 8 figs., 35 tables in text.

GETTY, H.T. 1935. New dates from Mesa Verde. Tree-ring Bulletin, 1(3):21-23.

HOFFMEISTER, D.F. 1951. A taxonomic and evolutionary study of the piyon mouse, Peromyscus truei. Illinois Biol. Monogr., vol. XXI(4), pp. ix + 104, 24 figs., 4 tables and 5 plates in text.

RODECK, H.G. and ANDERSON, S. 1956. Sorex merriami and Microtus mexicanus in Colorado. Jour. Mamm., 37(3):436.

SCHULMAN, E. 1946. Dendrochronology at Mesa Verde National Park. Tree-ring Bulletin, 12(3):18-24, 2 figs., 1 table in text.

YOUNGMAN, P.M. 1958. Geographic variation in the pocket gopher, Thomomys bottae, in Colorado. Univ. Kansas Publ., Mus. Nat. Hist., 9(12):363-387, 7 figs. in text.

Transmitted April 11, 1961.

UNIVERSITY OF KANSAS PUBLICATIONS MUSEUM OF NATIONAL HISTORY

Institutional libraries interested in publications exchange may obtain this series by addressing the Exchange Librarian, University of Kansas Library, Lawrence, Kansas. Copies for individuals, persons working in a particular field of study, may be obtained by addressing instead the Museum of Natural History, University of Kansas, Lawrence, Kansas. There is no provision for sale of this series by the University Library, which meets institutional requests, or by the Museum of Natural History, which meets the requests of individuals. However, when individuals request copies from the Museum, 25 cents should be included, for each separate number that is 100 pages or more in length, for the purpose of defraying the costs of wrapping and mailing.

* An asterisk designates those numbers of which the Museum's supply (not the Library's supply) is exhausted. Numbers published to date, in this series, are as follows:

Vol. 1. Nos. 1-26 and index. Pp. 1-638, 1946-1950.

*Vol. 2. (Complete) Mammals of Washington. By Walter W. Dalquest. Pp. 1-444, 140 figures in text. April 9, 1948.

Vol. 3. *1. The avifauna of Micronesia, its origin, evolution, and distribution.

By Rollin H. Baker. Pp. 1-359, 16 figures in text. June 12, 1951.

*2. A quantitative study of the nocturnal migration of birds. By George H. Lowery, Jr. Pp. 361-472, 47 figures in text. June 29, 1951.

3. Phylogeny of the waxwings and allied birds. By M. Dale Arvey. Pp. 478-530, 49 figures in text, 18 tables. October 10, 1951.

4. Birds from the state of Veracruz, Mexico. By George H. Lowery, Jr., and Walter W. Dalquest. Pp. 531-649, 7 figures in text, 2 tables. October 10, 1951.

Index. Pp. 651-681.

*Vol. 4. (Complete) American weasels. By E. Raymond Hall. Pp. 1-466, 41 plates, 31 figures in text. December 27, 1951.

Vol. 5. Nos. 1-37 and index. Pp. 1-676, 1951-1953.

*Vol. 6. (Complete) Mammals of Utah, taxonomy and distribution. By Stephen D. Durrant. Pp. 1-549, 91 figures in text, 30 tables. August 10, 1952.

Vol. 7. *1. Mammals of Kansas. By E. Lendell Cockrum. Pp. 1-303, 73 figures in text, 37 tables. August 25, 1952.

2. Ecology of the opossum on a natural area in northeastern Kansas. By Henry S. Fitch and Lewis L. Sandidge. Pp. 305-338, 5 figures in text. August 24, 1953.

3. The silky pocket mice (Perognathus flavus) of Mexico. By Rollin H. Baker. Pp. 339-347, 1 figure in text. February 15, 1954.

4. North American jumping mice (Genus Zapus). By Philip H. Krutzsch. Pp. 349-472, 47 figures in text, 4 tables, April 21, 1954.

5. Mammals from Southeastern Alaska. By Rollin H. Baker and James S. Findley. Pp. 473-477. April 21, 1954.

6. Distribution of Some Nebraskan Mammals. By J. Knox Jones, Jr. Pp. 479-487. April 21, 1954.

7. Subspeciation in the montane meadow mouse. Microtus montanus, in Wyoming and Colorado. By Sydney Anderson. Pp. 489-506, 2 figures in text. July 23, 1954.

8. A new subspecies of bat (Myotis velifer) from southeastern California and Arizona. By Terry A. Vaughan. Pp. 507-512. July 28, 1954.

9. Mammals of the San Gabriel mountains of California. By Terry A. Vaughan. Pp. 513-582, 1 figure in text, 12 tables. November 15, 1954.

10. A new bat (Genus Pipistrellus) from northeastern Mexico. By Rollin H. Baker. Pp. 583-586. November 15, 1954.

11. A new subspecies of pocket mouse from Kansas. By E. Raymond Hall. Pp. 587-590. November 15, 1954.

12. Geographic variation in the pocket gopher, Cratogeomys castanops, in Coahuila, Mexico. By Robert J. Russell and Rollin H. Baker. Pp. 591-608. March 15, 1955.

13. A new cottontail (Sylvilagus floridanus) from northeastern Mexico. By Rollin H. Baker. Pp. 609-612. April 8, 1955.

14. Taxonomy and distribution of some American shrews. By James S. Findley. Pp. 613-618. June 10, 1955.

15. The pigmy woodrat, Neotoma goldmani, its distribution and systematic position. By Dennis G. Rainey and Rollin H. Baker. Pp. 619-624, 2 figures in

text. June 10, 1955.

Index. Pp. 625-651.

Vol. 8. Nos. 1-10 and index. Pp. 1-675, 1954-1956.

Vol. 9. 1. Speciation of the wandering shrew. By James S. Findley. Pp. 1-68, 18 figures in text. December 10, 1955.

2. Additional records and extensions of ranges of mammals from Utah. By Stephen D. Durrant, M. Raymond Lee, and Richard M. Hansen. Pp. 69-80. December 10, 1955.

3. A new long-eared myotis (Myotis evotis) from northeastern Mexico. By Rollin H. Baker and Howard J. Stains. Pp. 81-84. December 10, 1955.

4. Subspeciation in the meadow mouse, Microtus pennsylvanicus, in Wyoming. By Sydney Anderson. Pp. 85-104, 2 figures in text. May 10, 1956.

5. The condylarth genus Ellipsodon. By Robert W. Wilson. Pp. 105-116, 6 figures in text. May 19, 1956.

6. Additional remains of the multituberculate genus Eucosmodon. By Robert W. Wilson. Pp. 117-123, 10 figures in text. May 19, 1956.

7. Mammals of Coahuila, Mexico. By Rollin H. Baker, Pp. 125-335, 75 figures in text. June 15, 1956.

8. Comments on the taxonomic status of Apodemus peninsulae, with description of a new subspecies from North China. By J. Knox Jones, Jr. Pp. 337-346, 1 figure in text, 1 table. August 15, 1956.

9. Extensions of known ranges of Mexican bats. By Sydney Anderson. Pp. 347-351. August 15, 1956.

Jr. Pp. 213-552, 34 plates, 8 figures in text, 35 tables. November 7, 1958.

7. Home ranges and movements of the eastern cottontail in Kansas. By Donald W. Janes. Pp. 558-572, 4 plates, 3 figures in text. May 4, 1959.

8. Natural history of the salamander, Aneides hardyi. By Richard F. Johnston and Schad Gerhard. Pp. 573-585. October 8, 1959.

9. A new subspecies of lizard, Cnemidophorus sacki, from Michoac 醬, Mexico. By William E. Duellman. Pp. 587-598, 2 figures in text. May 2, 1960.

10. A taxonomic study of the Middle American Snake, Pituophis deppei. By William E. Duellman. Pp. 599-612, 1 plate, 1 figure in text. May 2, 1960.

Index Pp. 611-626.

Vol. 11. 1. The systematic status of the colubrid snake, Leptodeira discolor. By William E. Duellman. Pp. 1-9, 4 figs. July 14, 1958.

2. Natural history of the six-lined racerunner, Cnemidophorus sexlineatus. By Henry S. Fitch. Pp. 11-62. 9 figs., 9 tables. September 19, 1958.

3. Home ranges, territories, and seasonal movements of vertebrates of the Natural History Reservation. By Henry S. Fitch. Pp. 63-326, 6 plates, 24 figures in text, 3 tables. December 12, 1958.

4. A new snake of the genus Geophis from Chihuahua, Mexico. By John M. Legler. Pp. 327-334, 2 figures in text. January 28, 1959.

5. A new tortoise, genus Gopherus, from north-central Mexico. By John M. Legler. Pp. 335-343. April 24, 1959.

6. Fishes of Chautauqua, Cowley and Elk counties, Kansas. By Artie L. Metcalf. Pp. 345-400, 2 plates, 2 figures in text, 10 tables. May 6, 1959.

7. Fishes of the Big Blue River Basin, Kansas. By W.L. Minckley, Pp. 401-442, 2 plates, 4 figures in text, 5 tables. May 8, 1959.

8. Birds from Coahuila, Mexico. By Emil K. Urban. Pp. 443-516. August 1, 1959.

9. Description of a new softshell turtle from the southeastern United States. By Robert G. Webb. Pp. 517-525, 2 pls., 1 figure in text. August 14, 1959.

10. Natural history of the ornate box turtle, Terrapene ornata ornata Agassiz. By John M. Legler. Pp. 527-669, 16 pls., 29 figures in text. March 7, 1960.

Index Pp. 671-703.

Vol. 12. 1. Functional morphology of three bats: Eumops, Myotis, Macrotus. By Terry A. Vaughan. Pp. 1-153, 4 plates, 24 figures in text. July 8, 1959.

2. The ancestry of modern Amphibia: a review of the evidence. By Theodore H. Eaton, Jr. Pp. 155-180, 10 figures in text. July 10, 1959.

3. The baculum in microtine rodents. By Sydney Anderson. Pp. 181-216, 49 figures in text. February 19, 1960.

4. A new order of fishlike Amphibia from the Pennsylvanian of Kansas. By Theodore H. Eaton, Jr., and Peggy Lou Stewart. Pp. 217-240, 12 figures in text. May 2, 1960.

More numbers will appear in volume 12.

Vol. 13. 1. Five natural hybrid combinations in minnows (Cyprinidae). By Frank B. Cross and W.L. Minckley. Pp. 1-18. June 1, 1960.

2. A distributional study of the amphibians of the isthmus of Tehuantepec,

Mexico. By William E. Duellman. Pp. 19-72, pls. 1-8, 3 figs. August 16, 1960.

3. A new subspecies of the slider turtle (Pseudemys scripta) from Coahuila, Mexico. By John M. Legler. Pp. 73-84, pls. 9-12, 3 figures in text. August 16, 1960.

4. Autecology of the Copperhead. By Henry S. Fitch. Pp. 85-288, pls. 13-20, 26 figures in text. November 30, 1960.

5. Occurrence of the Garter Snake, Thamnophis sirtalis, in the Great Plains and Rocky Mountains. By Henry S. Fitch and T. Paul Maslin. Pp. 289-308, 4 figures in text. February 10, 1961.

6. Fishes of the Wakarusa River in Kansas. By James E. Deacon and Artie L. Metcalf. Pp. 309-32 2, 1 figure in text. February 10, 1961.

7. Geographic variation in the North American Cyprinid Fish, Hybopsis gracilis. By Leonard J. Olund and Frank B. Cross. Pp. 323-348, pls. 21-24, 2 figures in text. February 10, 1961.

8. Descriptions of two species of frogs, Genus Ptychohyla--studies of American hylid frogs, V. By William E. Duellman. Pp. 349-357, pls. 25, 2 figures in text. April 27, 1961.

More numbers will appear in volume 13.

Vol. 14. 1. Neotropical bats from western Mexico. By Sydney Anderson. Pp. 1-8. October 24, 1960.

2. Geographic variation in the harvest mouse Reithrodontomys megalotis on the central Great Plains and in adjacent regions. By J. Knox Jones, Jr. and B. Mursaloglu. Pp. 9-27, 1 figure in text. July 24, 1961.

3. Mammals of Mesa Verde National Park, Colorado. By Sydney Anderson.

Pp. 29-67, pls. 1-2, 3 figures in text. July 24, 1961.

More numbers will appear in volume 14.